Maria Theresia Bitterli & Dawio Bordoli

AF237683

Miracles, Siddhis and paranormal phenomena

Questions and answers with Ishvara

First edition 2020

© Studio Ishvara

Translated by Alex Dawson

Picture of Tumisu

studioishvara@hotmail.com

BoD – Books on Demand,

Norderstedt

ISBN: 9783751933575

Summary

Introduction

In Wikipedia a miracle is defined (from the Latin "miraculum", a wonderful thing) as an extraordinary event, above the natural laws, which is considered to be operated directly by God or through one of his creatures. A miracle is defined as an extraordinary event that takes place outside the laws of nature or in which natural laws appear suspended, by supernatural or divine intervention. In common parlance, it is often seen as an inexplicable or believed to be an impossible but positive event.

Miracles (from the Latin mirari, "to look with amazement") are present in almost all religions, but especially in Christianity which bases the Gospel message on the essence of the supernatural.

Many miracles performed by Jesus Christ are mentioned in the New Testament, such as the multiplication of the bread loaves and fishes or the healing of the sick, but the most important miracle is his own resurrection.

In Judaism, a miracle is a sign of God's omnipotence and of his benevolence towards the chosen people, particularly frequent in the days of the exodus from Egypt.

In Islam, miracles are considered signs of God's omnipotence.

Numerous events considered miraculous are recorded in the Old Testament. Two of these in particular, the exodus from Egypt and the division of the waters of the Red Sea, have become symbols of all the liberations that took place by divine work in history, and the theme of a large Jewish literature.

In the Gospels, miracles are signs of the mission of Christ, which will then be continued by the apostles and disciples.

The doctrine of the Church recognizes the miracle in the broader context of the history of salvation as a call for men.

Hinduism[1] classifies miracles and gives examples of them in its mythology and in the lives of hundreds of saints. A Siddhar is one who has siddhis, supernatural powers. These powers can be innate or achieved through austerity and mystical practices (sadhana). Despite the heavenly nature of siddhis, they are

---

[1] http://www.oltre.online/2016/02/12/i-miracoli-indu-e-scienza-yogica-ashta-ma-siddhis/

considered very dangerous for spiritual aspirants, given the extreme ease with which the development of these powers can lead to a growth of the ego, pride and vanity, qualities that hinder the path of the aspirant towards the ultimate goal of self-realization, enlightenment, Nirvana or Samadhi. The supreme siddhi (parasiddhi), superior to all others, is the realization of the Self.

Rationalist philosophers[2], especially David Hume, decidedly attacked the very concept of miracle. Indeed, Hume stated that a miracle would be a violation of ordinary natural laws and therefore impossible. However, it is possible that an event could be considered miraculous because man at that moment did not have a full and exhaustive knowledge of the laws of nature that regulate it. In fact, therefore,

---

[2] http://tanogabo.com/il-miracolo-nelle-varie-religioni/

to appeal to a miracle would simply be an admission of ignorance. As Spinoza already indicated that the reference to the divine will was nothing more than an excuse for the limits of our knowledge. The point of view of contemporary science, which cannot speak of a miracle, but simply a fact, for which the laws that allow it to happen are not known yet. Science in any case rejects the possibility of a supernatural intervention and therefore the concept itself of miracle.

Since science demands and pursues a full and exhaustive knowledge of reality, it cannot admit external intervention, outside of nature.

The problem of a miracle, of divine intervention, therefore, poses the same problems as free will and the mind-body (or mind-brain) problem, specifically how non-material causality is possible.

In this book you will find some events considered supernatural which have been further investigated by asking questions to Ishvara.

The mind deceives us[3]

The scientist works as a detective, makes assumptions and then draws conclusions, as Italian psychologist Massimio Polidoro explained. But there is a whole series of mysteries that science, on the other hand, does not face.

The brain, that is an extraordinary machine, deceives us every now and then by showing us only what is in our imagination. The classic case is that of the shapes of clouds or spots on a wall. This phenomenon is called Pareidolia. "It is that mechanism that leads us to recognize faces or faces on some images. An American lady saw a face on a burned toast slice, she thought it was Our Lady, she put it on ebay collecting 20 thousand dollars. In short, a prodigy can be built on nothing".

---

[3] https://www.focus.it/cultura/mistero/come-e-perche-la-mente-ci-inganna-polidoro

Very often we believe what we want to believe. "We find ourselves talking to like-minded people who strengthen our beliefs. Denying hoaxes, removing illusions, for example, that a cure is a scam for many is unacceptable. But if we want to evolve, we must know, and knowledge brings uncertainties. "

For sure the more we know, the more questions we ask ourselves. Science, concludes Polidoro, is a method of knowing reality. Einstein said: "All our science in comparison with reality is primitive and childish, but it is the most precious thing we have".

The mind makes a lot of jokes. We often project images that are not really real.
We happened to find ourselves in a group of people, both composed of scientists and spiritual seekers, with

whom we met to meditate. We were convinced that we had seen a "particular" light on a mountain and that, after going to check, unfortunately we found that it was just a lamppost!

What exactly happens in such a situation?
Ishvara: This is collective conscious autosuggestion.

What is a collective conscious autosuggestion?
Ishvara: A sensory vision perceived by several people.

How is it possible that such brilliant minds have been deceived by a collective conscious autosuggestion?
Ishvara: Illusions deceive even the brightest minds.

How can we protect ourselves from illusions?
Ishvara: Discarding what is not real.

Is there always something we miss? Can we not completely distinguish true from false?

Ishvara: Start looking for truth somewhere.

There is a lot of information about miracles but understanding which ones are true is very difficult. This can also be counterproductive because this jungle means that when we are faced with authentic supernatural phenomena, we miss or not believe them. It seems almost impossible to transmit extraordinary events as ordinary.

Ishvara: The repeatability of an event does not make it more miraculous.

If a miracle occurs again, is the interest of the event lost?

Ishvara: This is the reaction of a common mind.

Are there any miraculous events that repeat themselves and that always manage to involve people? For instance, spontaneous healings or visions of Mother Mary?

Ishvara: The "always" is out of place.

Are people always looking for new stimuli?

Ishvara: Yes, like children.

The magnetic hills[4]

A strange phenomenon arouses curiosity in mystery fans. We refer to the so-called magnetic hills. These are those places that give the feeling that gravity is absent or strongly altered compared to normal. In these areas, for example, a car left in neutral on an uphill road, instead of going down as it would be logical continues to go upwards as attracted by a mysterious magnetic force. In the past, various theories have been formulated about this phenomenon. For example, there have been those who spoke of a phantom alteration of the gravitational field.

---

[4] https://www.notizieora.it/lo-strano-caso-delle-colline-magnetiche-ecco-in-cosa-consiste-il-curioso-fenomeno/

Is this phenomenon connected to spirits? Does the gravitational field have anything to do with it? Or is it simply an optical illusion?

Ishvara: It is a variation of the gravitational field.

What happens when there is a change in the gravitational field?

Ishvara: All living systems undergo a variation of different scope.

What influence do these phenomena have on Earth or the Multiverse?

Ishvara: They affect every single subatomic cell.

What would this mean for human beings?

Ishvara: Changes of all kinds.

What types of changes could happen?

Ishvara: Natural catastrophes of all kinds.

Was this phenomenon manipulated by humans or is it something that happens naturally?

Ishvara: All naturally.

Could it also have a naturalistic catastrophic influence such as storms, volcanic eruptions, earthquakes or tsunamis, etc. ...?

Ishvara: It could be a trigger.

Could being in such a place also have a negative influence on one's health?

Ishvara: It will depend on each individual.

What type of individuals are at risk?

Ishvara: Those with serious health problems.

Why are there such phenomena? Of what use are they to Earth?

Ishvara: They serve to rebalance the entire system.

Are they like relief valves?

Ishvara: Yes.

Does 5G also affect the gravitational field and could it have a negative influence on living systems?

Ishvara: It subjects your organism to greater stress.

Do extraterrestrials also have a connection with the phenomenon of magnetic hills?

Ishvara: Sometimes they use them as terrestrial intervention bases.

Telekinesis or Psychokinesis [5]

The word psychokinesis derives from Greek; it consists in the union of the words psyche - psycho (soul) and kinesis (movement); often abbreviated to PK (psychokinesis) or TK (telekinesis). It is also known as Telekinesis, ie action at a distance and consists in the ability of a living being (generally a human) to act on the surrounding environment in ways unknown to science; in common language it is used to say 'by the power of thought'. The scholars who are interested in it, the parapsychologists, distinguish two categories: Macro-Psychokinesis and Micro-Psychokinesis.

The first involves phenomena directly observable with the naked eye, for example the movement of objects or the levitation of the medium itself; Micro-

---

[5] http://www.inspiegabile.com/paranormale/fenomeni-parapsicologia-telecinesi-psicocinesi.html

Psychokinesis, on the other hand, consists of phenomena not directly observable such as alterations of objects at the molecular level and small increases in their temperature, changes of the magnetic fields or the intervention in probabilistic phenomena.

Is it really possible that people can move objects with the mind?

Ishvara: Yes.

How does it work?

Ishvara: First learn to meditate, then you can get closer.

Can objects be moved by themselves?

Ishvara: No.

Who or what moves them?

Ishvara: Gravity.

Could an object on a table be moved by an entity?

Ishvara: Of course.

Does an entity therefore act on Gravity and the energy field to generate the movement of an object?

Ishvara: It is the cause.

And in the case of levitation?

Ishvara: It is a voluntary action on gravity.

What do you mean by voluntary action?

Ishvara: Someone who acts.

Are there any tricks?

Ishvara: Yes.

Are there also cheaters?

Ishvara: Yes.

Are there any particular meditation techniques to achieve telekinesis or psychokinesis?

Ishvara: Yes, it takes a lot of discipline.

Are they the ones that Shaolin monks use for example?

Ishvara: Yes.

With these techniques, can objects be materialized and dematerialized from one dimension to another?

Ishvara: Yes.

Can it also happen in a non-voluntary way?

Ishvara: No. Not knowing its cause doesn't mean it's involuntary.

What happens if the television, radio or computer turns on or off by itself?

Ishvara: The causes will vary from time to time.

If it is not a technical issue, could it be an action done by entities?

Ishvara: Yes.

Are they entities of the lower astral?

Ishvara: Often.

Why?

Ishvara: Evolved beings rarely use these ways.

Could it also be the force of the mind that turns appliances on or off?

Ishvara: There is always a being behind the mind.

Do evolved beings use light to communicate instead?

Ishvara: No.

Why does a light turn on and off unintentionally?

Ishvara: They might be making fun of you.

And when you hear a knock on a windows or door radiators? Are they always beings of the lower astral?

Ishvara: Almost always.

And when a heavy table is moved during a seance, how does it work?

Ishvara: Someone does an action for such purpose.

Here too, are they beings of the lower astral?

Ishvara: The difference is the type of message sent.

Could evolved beings use all these means if they are meant to teach us something?

Ishvara: Yes, but they are more direct.

Where do the objects that dematerialize from our dimension go to?

Ishvara: On other planes of existence.

What is the purpose of such an object in other dimensions?

Ishvara: The purpose is always to teach something.

Any object that materializes in our dimension has the purpose of teaching us something and when the purpose has been achieved will it be dematerialized again?

Ishvara: Not necessarily.

Why not?

Ishvara: Because it could be used as a simple cult object.

UFOs and extraterrestrials[6]

Are we really alone in the Universe? Today, there are increasing number of people who believe that we are not alone. But there are those who believe, and those who do not believe. Yet in recent times UFO sightings have multiplied and strange signs appear in the skies.

But, beyond the legends, myths and texts of religious traditions, it is with the documented history that the path becomes as fascinating and fraught with questions, from the enigmatic presences recorded in the Renaissance to the fascist dossiers, from the secret archives of the KGB to those of the Pentagon.

So, can we talk about alien visitors? Reality or imagination?

---

[6]http://www.acam.it/extraterrestri/

Ishvara: A lot of imagination and some reality yet to be discovered.

Conspiracy or misinformation?

Ishvara: They are connected, but there is reality.

Are there no more doubts that there are extraterrestrials among us?

Ishvara: There are, but not everyone will believe it.

But why are they still hiding?

Ishvara: Because there are still too many fears.

By analogy, the same could be said, for example, in the case of new refugees. Not knowing their culture and seeing them different, people avoid them and are afraid of them. So, it was with the Turks, with the Italians and other cultures. So, it will be with the extraterrestrials. Will they have to come forward sooner or later?

Ishvara: They have already come forward with a few of you.

How come?

Ishvara: To convey technological knowledge.

Is this why we have evolved technologically in such a short time?

Ishvara: Yes.

So, are they in touch with people who already have technological knowledge such as artificial intelligence?

Ishvara: Yes.

Isn't there a risk that their knowledge will be used for not so evolved purposes?

Ishvara: That's why they are transmitted with caution.

How do they communicate with us?

Ishvara: Essentially telepathically.

So, they don't know our languages, do they?

Ishvara: They use a more efficient system.

Are some of them born on Earth?

Ishvara: Yes.

So, are there already cases of procreation between extraterrestrials and us humans?

Ishvara: Yes.

Do they procreate like us?

Ishvara: Yes.

Why are they on Earth too?

Ishvara: To evolve.

Are there any threatening extraterrestrials to us?

Ishvara: In rare cases.

How do we recognize the good guys from the bad guys?

Ishvara: With the same human criteria.

If they have already procreated with us, do they also know our languages?

Ishvara: Those closest to your species.

Are extraterrestrials smarter than us?

Ishvara: Yes.

Why do they want to experiment on us?

Ishvara: To help you.

How so?

Ishvara: Making you evolve.

Is it one of their tasks to make us evolve?

Ishvara: It's the main task.

Are they always in touch with their home planets?

Ishvara: Not always.

Why not always?

Ishvara: Because they have other things to do.

Do they have to earn their living like us?

Ishvara: Yes, because they live in the same economic system.

So, there are extraterrestrials integrated with us and others on spaceships, correct?

Ishvara: Yes, and others on various planets.

Are we afraid of those who live on spaceships?

Ishvara: This is up to you to say it.

Can those who live on the various planets study us and observe us from there?

Ishvara: Yes.

Could any of us humans go and live on their planets?

Ishvara: Yes.

Would they be aware that they moved to another planet?

Ishvara: At first, they will be stunned, then the new reality will be accepted.

How did they integrate on the new planet?

Ishvara: Accompanied by competent guides.

Are their planets much different from ours?

Ishvara: It depends from planet to planet.

Since they communicate in a telepathic way and their technology is very advanced and certainly silent, will it be very quiet to live with them?

Ishvara: They don't get lost in useless chatter.

Are they also interested in a spiritual journey?

Ishvara: Much more than you.

So, thanks to advanced technology like robotics, they have enough free time to devote to spiritual development, isn't it?

Ishvara: Just like it is happening to you.

Is that what's going on now with covid-19?

Ishvara: Everything is in strong acceleration.

Could they be our future spiritual masters?

Ishvara: Only for some of you.

Are they vegan?

Ishvara: Yes, too.

Does it depend on the state of consciousness?

Ishvara: Yes, and by individual sensitivity.

Are there any extraterrestrials that are particularly evolved and sensitive to animals?

Ishvara: Yes.

Do they also have diseases or are they so advanced that they are always healthy?

Ishvara: They also have them.

Do they also do sports to keep fit?

Ishvara: Of course.

Do they do activities we don't know about?

Ishvara: Yes.

How long can an extraterrestrial live?

Ishvara: Even beyond 7000 years.

Does a year of their life correspond to a year of our life?

Ishvara: The comparison is similar.

But how many hours of sleep do they need?

Ishvara: None, since they self-regenerate.

Does self-regeneration take place through meditation?

Ishvara: Yes.

How many hours do they meditate per day?

Ishvara: 24 hours.

Do they use a particular technique?

Ishvara: Constant self-observation.

What is the biggest difference between a human being and extraterrestrials?

Ishvara: It will depend from case to case.

And what do we have in common?

Ishvara: The Source.

Could it be an enrichment to get to know each other better and to grow in parallel?

Ishvara: It is desirable.

Will it still take a long time to get to this point?

Ishvara: Everything will happen quickly in future years.

How will our collaboration with them be?

Ishvara: Very profitable for all humanity and the whole world.

The Bermuda Triangle[7]

The Bermuda Triangle is an area of a million square kilometers in the middle of the Atlantic Ocean shrouded in a great mystery: ships and planes have disappeared throughout history without leaving a trace.

The discovery of a missing ship in an area outside the notorious triangle in late November 1925 inflicts the mystery of the devil's triangle. There have been several theories related to this mystery but now it seems that all the fantasies that have been created are falling.

Are we still faced with a mystery?

Ishvara: Part of it still remains a mystery.

---

[7] https://www.reccom.org/2020/02/17/triangolo-delle-bermuda-nuovo-colpo-alla-teoria-cospirazionista-ritrovata-la-nave-cotopaxi-scomparsa-nel-1925/

Is this a portal for UFOs?

Ishvara: It has been and will be in the years to come.

Where have all the planes, ships, etc. gone?

Ishvara: In parallel worlds.

So, are we in front of a portal to parallel worlds?

Ishvara: Yes.

Did people survive?

Ishvara: Yes.

Are they still in the same body?

Ishvara: No.

Did they change form when they were teleported?

Ishvara: Yes, they left the old form.

Are they not aware of the change experienced?

Ishvara: They are each aware in their own way.

Do UFOs and extraterrestrials use this portal to move from this dimension to another?

Ishvara: Yes, they are accesses to other dimensions.

What is this triangle for?

Ishvara: To rebalance the planet.

Just like the magnetic hills?

Ishvara: Through magnetic storms.

How do magnetic storms work?

Ishvara: They start from solar flares.

Do solar flares have negative consequences on Earth?

Ishvara: Yes.

What could happen in the worst-case scenario?

Ishvara: The largest solar flares could cause an electrical blackout with catastrophic consequences for humanity and nature.

What do solar flares mainly depend on?

Ishvara: On the sun's self-regeneration.

Regarding the aforementioned ship that was found, why hasn't it teleported?

Ishvara: It teleported for some time.

So, did people find themselves with the ship in other waters?

Ishvara: Yes, but not for all.

Why?

Ishvara: Karmic reasons.

Did others die then?

Ishvara: No.

Nobody died?

Ishvara: Yes.

How come the ship then returned to this dimension?

Ishvara: To be found and documented.

But then the theories we talked about will fall?

Ishvara: They integrate.

And what about those who don't believe in this integration process?

Ishvara: We can't deal with them now.

Who should we deal with instead?

Ishvara: With those who are willing to question themselves.

In the aforementioned case, what function do extraterrestrials have for people who are teleported?
Ishvara: They accompany them.

Where to?
Ishvara: In other spatio-temporal dimensions.

What can you tell us about the pyramid at the bottom of the Bermuda Triangle?
Ishvara: It is a cosmic antenna.

What is it for?
Ishvara: To stabilize Earth's magnetism.

Who built it?

Ishvara: Extraterrestrials.

What was it for them?

Ishvara: As a base for spaceships.

Crop circles[8]

Crop circles have complex geometric shapes, difficult to achieve even with the drafting machine and a compass in hand. They can reach a width of several tens, and in some cases hundreds of meters. They arise suddenly, in a matter of hours or in a night, tracing perfect circles of flattened crops, inside which there are designs of varying complexity and great precision.

There are testimonies of similar apparitions dating back to 1678, then considered "the work of the devil", but in recent years the phenomenon has been intensifying, both quantitatively and qualitatively, with the creation of increasingly elaborate models. Most of the apparitions are located in the south of

---

[8] https://www.lifegate.it/persone/stile-di-vita/i_cerchi_nel_grano1

England, although there is no lack of reports in other parts of world.

However, the increase in interest and study of the phenomenon has not helped to shed light on its real nature. Who is responsible for these works?

Ishvara: In most cases extraterrestrial forms.

Do they create them with spaceships? How can they do such a thing in no time?

Ishvara: From spaceships.

Are they formed when they land with their spaceships?

Ishvara: They don't need to land.

Are the symbols they create messages for us?

Ishvara: They are energetic mandalas.

So, they create them to rebalance a certain place?

Ishvara: Yes, too.

What else are they useful for?

Ishvara: For the psyche of those who contemplate them.

Do they therefore also have a healing function?

Ishvara: Yes.

How come do they appear more in the south of England?

Ishvara: Greater availability of people.

Are others afraid?

Ishvara: The majority.

Extraterrestrials have good intentions but are not understood by us humans, isn't it?

Ishvara: They will know how to deserve your trust.

What could they do to decrease our fears?

Ishvara: Show themselves more and more.

Do they look like us?

Ishvara: Some do.

Are they as they show us on TV?

Ishvara: Also.

What is particular about them?

Ishvara: There are too many characteristics that differentiate them according to their planetary origin.

How will we recognize them when they show up more and more?

Ishvara: You will understand it without any doubt.

Are these crop circles their gifts?

Ishvara: Yes.

Do crop circles also have the function of purifying the environment?

Ishvara: Yes, they re-balance at a general level.

Are crop circles also another way of getting noticed?

Ishvara: Yes.

Deep knowledge is hidden in these crop circles which is a gift on their part, isn't it?

Ishvara: They have a positive effect on the mind of the beholder.

So, are all these theories about their meaning incorrect?

Ishvara: Theories don't always correspond to facts.

How do we understand which theories are reliable?

Ishvara: Making direct experience.

Contemplating the image?

Ishvara: Yes, meditating on it.

And is this how new visions, perceptions and intuitions about our world and the Multiverse open up to us?

Ishvara: Consciousness will expand to new horizons.

So, is it advisable to be open to their future mandalas?

Ishvara: Openness of heart and mind is of fundamental importance.

Is this also a way for us to prepare for the official arrival of extraterrestrials on Earth?

Ishvara: Yes.

The living rocks of Romania[9]

In Romania, 35 kilometers from Ramnicu Valcea, exceptional rocks have been discovered, able to grow and reproduce just as if they were plants, reacting on contact with water.

The Trovants, that's what they are called, have characteristics so unique that they are considered "live" rocks. Formations of 6-8 millimeters, can form on rocks from 6 to 10 meters in diameter. Stunning growth, even if in very long timespan: on average, for a growth of 5 centimeters it takes 1200 years.

Where do these rocks come from?

Ishvara: From the Multiverse.

---

[9] https://www.lastampa.it/viaggi/mondo/2018/01/14/news/scoperte-in-romania-delle-pietre-in-grado-di-crescere-e-riprodursi-1.33967347

Does that mean they don't all come from the same place?

Ishvara: Many are the planets they come from.

Who put them on Earth?

Ishvara: Extraterrestrials.

For what reason?

Ishvara: To regenerate Earth.

How do they regenerate it?

Ishvara: They give off an energy field that reproduces them and that helps Earth maintain a magnetic balance.

Why are they alive, reproducing and moving?

Ishvara: To best perform their function of rebalancing terrestrial magnetism.

Do they adapt to the energy field by moving?

Ishvara: Growing up, they tumble.

What do they have in common with the stones of the Death Valley in America?

Ishvara: The function is the same.

Is it the source that changes?

Ishvara: The planets of origin.

Do extraterrestrials work together for the good of the Earth?

Ishvara: Yes.

Are they basically peaceful to each other?

Ishvara: Yes, there is the law of non-interference.

Are all the stones alive?

Ishvara: Yes.

Do spirits live there?

Ishvara: Yes.

What types of spirits?

Ishvara: Any type.

What types of spirits are there on Machu Picchu?

Ishvara: Passed away shamans.

What function do they have?

Ishvara: They are carrying out sacred ceremonies to safeguard Pachamama.

What secret is hidden on Machu Picchu?

Ishvara: It was an extraterrestrial base.

Don't they use it anymore now?

Ishvara: Currently it has only a planetary energetic value.

Was it prepared by extraterrestrials?

Ishvara: Yes.

Is there a relationship between the Trovants and Machu Picchu?

Ishvara: They interact to maintain the Earth's magnetic balance.

Are there Trovants there as well?

Ishvara: Of course.

Have they already discovered them?

Ishvara: They are deep underground.

What is still hidden in the subsoil?

Ishvara: Many beings that you will discover in the future.

Unexplained disappearances in Yellowstone park[10]

A series of strange circumstances seem to unite all these cases of people who for no apparent reason vanish into thin air, every year American national parks are visited by thousands of hikers and tourists of which hundreds of them never return.

Most of these disappearances can be attributed to accidents such as falling from cliffs or after being swallowed up by the strong currents of the rivers, moreover it cannot be excluded that their disappearance may find an explanation attributable to an attack by wild animals who would devour its bodies.

---

[10] http://www.mondotemporeale.net/2015/12/sparizioni-inspiegabili-nel-parco-dello_28.html

How come people disappear in the park?

Ishvara: Apart from various incidents, some cases have been drawn from extraterrestrials.

Are some people teleported to other dimensions?

Ishvara: Yes.

To do what?

Ishvara: Educate and prepare for future tasks.

Do most return to Earth?

Ishvara: No.

Do they disappear permanently without leaving a trace?

Ishvara: No, they are present in another form.

Would family members lose their loved one?

Ishvara: Any great mission requires putting the common good first to the individual and family good.

Are missing people following a great Mission?
Ishvara: Absolutely yes.

What great things do they do for example?
Ishvara: They return under other guises on Earth to help humanity evolve in the different disciplines.

What mystery is there in this national park?
Ishvara: Mysteries that will be revealed thanks to the arrival of extraterrestrials.

Will they soon be recognized by the whole world?
Ishvara: Yes.

Elemental beings on Earth[11]

The four basic elements of the Universe (in energetic and spiritual terms) are air, water, earth, and fire, and the human being is made up of these elements (which is a microcosm, a miniature universe); however, there are beings that we could define as semi-intelligent and that are made up of only one of the fundamental elements: the so-called Elemental Beings.

The first to study them was Paracelsus. These beings are made of the specific substance of each particular element, they have a permanent astral body and an etheric vehicle that they materialize at will (it is through this vehicle that they can be seen), they are defined "builders of form" because their specialty consists precisely in translating thought-forms into

---

[11] https://www.scienzenoetiche.it/raphael_project/inc_088.php

physical forms by transforming mental models into etheric and therefore into physical models, receiving orders from the higher Devas. Their shape depends on the influence of the archetype and the function to which they are subject, and also on the influence of human thought forms. Not infrequently these sprites of nature have fun imitating human beings, even in the way they dress. They live their activities with cheerfulness, joy and pleasure, and often elementals like to play jokes.

What are elemental beings useful for?

Ishvara: They are fundamental for nature.

How come they hide from us?

Ishvara: To protect themselves.

What could happen to them if we saw them?

Ishvara: They would run the risk of being destroyed.

Why should human beings want to destroy them?
Ishvara: For lack of empathy.

If we destroyed them, would we eliminate ourselves?
Ishvara: Yes.

How do elementals communicate with us?
Ishvara: With the same language.

What would they want to tell us if we listened to them?
Ishvara: To take better care of the Earth.

Are we responsible for covid-19?
Ishvara: And who else but you humans.

What have we mainly done wrong?

Ishvara: You underestimated the risks and overestimated your abilities.

What kind of risks?

Ishvara: For your health and that of Earth.

How could this happen?

Ishvara: Ignorance.

What about the ego and greed?

Ishvara: They are its children.

Could elementals also help us with this covid-19 virus?

Ishvara: Yes.

What went wrong in this regard?

Ishvara: Greater imbalances have been created between the elements.

Why are we undergoing such a situation?
Ishvara: Out of carelessness.

Now what will we have to do to fix it?
Ishvara: Reconnect to Mother Nature.

Should we then eliminate everything that disrupts the elements and Mother Earth?
Ishvara: Yes, through introspection.

What consequences would this have on us?
Ishvara: It would reconnect you to the elementals.

And could this lead us to collaborate with them?

Ishvara: They would help you find solutions to current problems.

Do elementals have the solution to covid-19 virus?
Ishvara: Yes.

How could they help us defeat it?
Ishvara: By accepting them and collaborating with them in the healing of the planet.

Should we try to do everything we can to minimize Earth pollution?
Ishvara: Yes.

The whole economy broadly contributes to land pollution. It seems like an impossible change.
Ishvara: Not for Mother Earth who regenerates herself even without your help.

Could planet Earth calmly get rid of us in order to survive, as it seems it is already doing now silently in this current emergency of covid-19?

Ishvara: Nature will have no problem getting rid of you and discarding you.

Will we still be able to restore an earthly balance?

Ishvara: Yes, but it will depend on your collective commitment.

Can elementals be regarded as ferrymen?

Ishvara: Yes, too.

In case they discard us, will the elementals ferry us to another dimension?

Ishvara: Not only that, but luckily you won't go that far.

Why can't we humans be empathetic to elementals and extraterrestrials?

Ishvara: Because you listen to fears.

Where do these fears come from?

Ishvara: From ignorance.

Is this a sign that we are not so advanced yet?

Ishvara: The evolutionary process continues.

With covid-19 are we called to evolve in order to survive this virus?

Ishvara: There is an urgency in this.

Should we go back to nature and give up some well-being a little?

Ishvara: The process of re-harmonization will not require any renunciation since everything will happen naturally.

So many people will lose some economic well-being and will have to let go of the superfluous?
Ishvara: You will be called to change your values.

Will many leave their physical bodies because they will no longer be in tune with the new order of things?
Ishvara: Yes.

Will meditation also happen naturally?
Ishvara: Yes, and this will also lead to unexpected changes.

What changes will happen naturally and effortlessly?

Ishvara: Your body and mind will adapt to natural changes.

So, will the 4 elements and the elementals find their natural and harmonious path again?

Ishvara: There will be a new balance.

Will human beings be more open towards the elementals and will respect them more in the future without wanting to destroy them, rather living in harmony with them?

Ishvara: Yes, and nothing will be as before.

Does everyone experience the current change differently?

Ishvara: Yes.

What happens to those that don't accept this change?

Ishvara: They will suffer the consequences.

What will be mainly different from the situation before covid-19?

Ishvara: Human and environmental values will take precedence over economic ones.

Naga fireballs[12]

The Mé Kông is the longest and most important river in Indochina, and one of the largest in Asia. It originates in Tibet and after a journey of about 4500 km flows into the South China Sea. Its waters bathe the shores of many towns, including Nong Khai (615 km from Bangkok). Here, every year, during a Full Moon Festival, which falls towards the end of October, something surreal happens: hundreds of spheres of light come out of the river and go up in the sky.

The Buddhist Lent lasts three months and ends on a full moon day in October, in memory of the night the Buddha died. The awakened one died in fact on a full moon night in Kusinara, exactly in the month of Karttika (October-November) of the Buddhist

---

[12] https://portalemisteri.altervista.org/blog/le-sfere-di-fuoco-naga-del-mekong/

calendar. This can only make the phenomenon even more suggestive.

According to the inhabitants of the area, the Naga were responsible for the phenomenon, a mythical rectiloid people who according to legend still live in the depth of the river (in Sanskrit "nag" means snake).

Are there Nagas?
Ishvara: Yes.

Are they snakes?
Ishvara: Yes.

Are they dangerous?
Ishvara: No.

Are they evolved snakes?

Ishvara: Yes.

What do they do?

Ishvara: They purify the Earth.

Does this phenomenon of fireballs really exist?

Ishvara: Yes.

Who are these spheres of fire?

Ishvara: Entities of light.

Are these spheres of fire connected to the Naga inhabitants?

Ishvara: Of course, they are part of a ceremony.

Are these spheres of fire part of a ceremony related to the death of the Buddha?

Ishvara: Exactly.

What exactly happens during the ceremony?

Ishvara: Ascending energy is released.

For what reason?

Ishvara: To increase the Earth's energy and allow the elevation of human consciousness.

Does this phenomenon affect all humanity?

Ishvara: Yes, every individual.

Are there other such phenomena in the world?

Ishvara: Of course.

Why did fairies choose a full moon in October once a year for the ceremony?

Ishvara: So was decided by the Buddha.

Namibia - The Fairy Circles[13]

Thousands of irregular circles dot the thin grass of the Namib desert. The satellite images and photos captured by drones show prairies riddled with holes, a wild and endless territory that seems hit by many small bombs. But a closer look is enough to realize that you are facing one of the most astonishing spectacles of nature, known to scientists as the "fairy circles". These are circular areas of variable diameter between 2 and 20 meters, apparently sterile, or devoid of vegetation, surrounded by rings of tall grass.

Today the mystery of the fairy circles may have been revealed. Nature magazine published the first results of a field research conducted by a team of researchers from Princeton University led by biologist Corina

---

[13] https://www.focus.it/cultura/mistero/svelato-il-mistero-dei-cerchi-delle-fate

Tarnita. According to US scientists, circular signs in the desert are the result of competition between insects and plants. In fact, "drawing" them would be the combined action of colonies of termites (Psammotermes allocerus), which live underground, in competition with local shrubs that try to develop on the surface. Tarnita explains: «In the past, some researchers had advanced the hypothesis that fairy circles were created thanks to a sort of self-regulation among the plants present in the sandy soil: the plants help the neighboring ones, but they are in competition with others more distant. Another hypothesis attributed, however, the appearance of these spots to the presence of animals, such as termites, ants and rodents, who live inside the circles and feed on the roots of plants.

What creates these fairy circles?

Ishvara: Elementals of nature.

Do fairies also have something to do with it?

Ishvara: It's really them.

Why do they create these circles?

Ishvara: They are discharges of terrestrial energy.

Does this mean that excess energy is expelled from the Earth through the circles?

Ishvara: Yes, to rebalance the cosmo-telluric energy.

How do fairies interfere?

Ishvara: They prepare the ground.

If the fairies did not do this ceremony, what consequences could there be for Earth?

Ishvara: For example, an increase in volcanic eruptions.

Are there any other fairy circles on Earth?

Ishvara: Yes.

The mystery of the eternal flame of New York[14]

For years, scientists believed that the "eternal" flame located behind a waterfall in New York's Chestnut Ridge County Park was kept alive by gas produced and coming from the rocks below, however researchers at Indiana University have discovered that those rocks do not produce enough heat to trigger the reaction needed to release the gas. This obviously means that something else feeds the mysterious flame, but no one yet has been able to say what it is.

Is this flame created by nature?

Ishvara: It comes from the world invisible to the human eye.

Is it a form of materialization then?

---

[14] https://alienifranoi.wordpress.com/2013/05/14/il-mistero-della-fiamma-eterna-di-new-york/

Ishvara: Yes.

What does this flame mean?

Ishvara: They are the elementals of fire.

What function do they have in this case?

Ishvara: They burn air pollution.

How does such a small flame purify the atmosphere?

Ishvara: The undines carry the information.

Why is it located near a waterfall?

Ishvara: To enhance its effect.

Are there thousands of eternal lights on Earth doing this type of work?

Ishvara: Yes, and most are found underground.

Do the elementals of the 4 elements primarily work underground to help maintain Earth's balance?

Ishvara: Yes, so they work more undisturbed.

If they worked on the surface would they be even more effective?

Ishvara: And how.

Is it up to us humans to be more open-hearted and connected to nature to be able to welcome them in the best way without hurting them?

Ishvara: Yes, it is essential for your survival.

Ghosts, paranormal entities, vampires, poltergeists[15]

Crunches in empty attics, the screeching of chains in old castles, objects that suddenly move on their own or are used as weapons against people or animals, drips of water from intact ceilings and without pipes, sudden fires in places without the presence of flammable material. This short list is part of what can be traced back to the poltergeists, a phenomenon still partially inexplicable whose name derives from the German words "geist" (spirit) and "poltern" (which makes noise, restless).

According to popular belief, the activity of the poltergeists would focus on a particular member of a

---

15

https://www.letturefantastiche.com/poltergeist_fantasmi_violenti_fenomeni_naturali_o_altro_ancora.html family living in the haunted place, in particular very young people, preferably teenagers. The purpose of these entities would be to persecute that person or even harm them if possible. The actions of the poltergeists would manifest themselves suddenly and just as suddenly they would cease in the presence of third parties with respect to the family to which the persecuted subject belongs.

Do ghosts, paranormal entities, vampires and poltergeists really exist or are they the result of our mind?

Ishvara: Many are authentic.

Why do they exist?

Ishvara: To regulate karmic matters.

Are they non-embodied beings who could take revenge until they find their peace?

Ishvara: In the worst cases.

Could they even kill someone?

Ishvara: Of course.

What could be done to avoid having to get to this point?

Ishvara: Protect yourself in case of aggression.

How can they attack us?

Ishvara: As you humans do.

How can we protect ourselves?

Ishvara: First by not looking for them and then repeating the Mantra "Om Namo Ishvaraya Namaha".

Could it also be that they are the ones who are looking for us to scare us and get noticed?

Ishvara: Yes, and it's up to you to dismiss them with the Mantra.

So even if there is something karmically suspended, they cannot have any power over us if we repeat the Mantra?

Ishvara: Exactly and beware not to forget it.

Could we rebalance what is karmically pending still in this life or should we wait for the next incarnation?

Ishvara: In every incarnation there is always a karmic residue.

With relational constellations, for example, can we anticipate a karmic dissolution if this is allowed by the divine plan?

Ishvara: Yes.

What are the places to avoid where there are all these forms of negative entities?

Ishvara: They can sneak anywhere.

Can they also be at our house while we sleep?

Ishvara: Especially in states of unconsciousness you are vulnerable.

And if anyone has a great sense of guilt, do they have easy access?

Ishvara: Weaknesses of all kinds can ease their aggressions.

Do they feed on conflicts of any kind?

Ishvara: Yes.

If we don't protect ourselves in time, does it become difficult to get rid of them like in a possession?

Ishvara: Yes, in extreme cases.

Is it advisable to avoid old houses where ghosts are said to be haunted?

Ishvara: Yes.

Could these houses be purified before going to live there?

Ishvara: Yes, if you are strong enough.

And if it were not so because we overestimated ourselves, what could happen then?

Ishvara: You may also have to leave the body.

Better, therefore, to listen to the signals that the universe is sending us. If we encounter particularly alarming situations, is it better to stay away and repeat the Mantra as a form of protection?

Ishvara: Yes, wisdom and common sense will help you.

Can poltergeists also infiltrate through television, the internet, mobile phones or any dark image?

Ishvara: It's more difficult.

Should malicious people who might be infected with dark entities be avoided?

Ishvara: Yes, if you are not strong.

What makes us really strong?

Ishvara: Remember the power of the Mantra.

There are people who work just like ghost hunters. Are these people strong enough to defeat them?

Ishvara: Yes, in most cases.

Could pretending that these dark entities are not there make them strong?

Ishvara: Ignoring them does not protect you.

Will meditating with the Mantra and raising one's frequency protect us?

Ishvara: Yes.

Can covid-19 be associated with a dark entity?

Ishvara: They are many entities of the lower astral.

How can we stop them?

Ishvara: With the Mantra.

The miracles of Padre Pio and the stigmata[16]

The story of Saint Pio of Pietralcina and the extraordinary episodes that occurred both during his life and after his death, have been known to the faithful who for years have venerated him all over the world and with ever greater devotion, ever since Pope John Paul II on 16 June 2002 raised him to the honor of the altars.

On his long journey to God, Padre Pio received the gift of non-ordinary phenomena: ecstasy, bilocation, love wounds to the heart, stigmata and transverberation, substantial signs of his immense love for the Lord.

The unknown miracles of the saint with the stigmata are reported by the many testimonies of conversions,

---

[16] https://www.padrepiodapietrelcina.com/stimmate-padre-pio/

miracles and graces obtained by people of all ages, until today.

Padre Pio is an example of a great soul. Is it this deep faith toward God that made him so special and extraordinary and that gave him great skills as a healer?

Ishvara: Faith and divine plan.

How do stigmata form?

Ishvara: They manifest from the subtle planes.

Could someone inflict wounds on other subtle planes that later manifest in this dimension too?

Ishvara: Yes, there are several ways.

What exactly are stigmata for?

Ishvara: To atone for the sins of the world.

Does a person with stigmata feel so much pain that it could become almost unbearable?

Ishvara: Yes, but it will always be bearable.

Are the stigmata a sign of a higher mission?

Ishvara: Yes.

How come people from other religions had stigmata?

Ishvara: Many religions know the stigmata.

Can stigmata be seen as a sign indicating a mission to help other people to free themselves from karmic burdens or sins?

Ishvara: Yes.

Did Padre Pio free people from very dark entities even from a distance?

Ishvara: Yes

Did Padre Pio have any other special qualities that we do not know?

Ishvara: Yes, not everything is known to you now.

What makes a person more special and miraculous than another?

Ishvara: What you believe about her or him.

Did Padre Pio become special because he managed to help many people get better?

Ishvara: Yes.

Did Padre Pio and all the other saints follow the example of Jesus, the way of love?

Ishvara: Yes, and other spiritual teachers.

Spiritual masters who know how to perform miracles are recognized in particular by their religious institutions. How could anyone not be recognized?

Ishvara: Spiritual masters are ordinary people who were discovered later on.

Only if it is written in the divine plan will spiritual masters be discovered, isn't it?

Ishvara: Yes, they are not interested in recognition.

Marian apparitions[17]

A Marian apparition is a supernatural aspect of the Blessed Virgin Mary. The figure often takes its name from the city where the apparition is reported.

Marian apparitions are sometimes repeated in the same place and for an extended period of time. Most of the Marian apparitions took place to one person or to a small group. Sometimes Marian apparitions are connected to the weeping statues of the Virgin Mary.

How is it possible for a statue to cry?

Ishvara: It is possible just like other miracles.

Could you explain, in the case of the crying statue, how it works?

---

[17] https://it.qwe.wiki/wiki/Marian_apparition

Ishvara: First it manifests on the etheric level and then physical.

What is the meaning of tears?
Ishvara: Suffering in general.

Are the tears made of amrita?
Ishvara: It is rare.

What are they made of?
Ishvara: Mostly blood.

Is it the blood of Jesus Christ?
Ishvara: Yes.

Does the statue really cry or is there a being of light that tears inside the statue?

Ishvara: The tear occurs first on a subtle level and then physical level.

Is it something then that appears on the statue and there is no real presence of the Virgin Mary?

Ishvara: The Virgin Mary is its primary manifestation.

In the sense that it is Our Lady who determines when, where and how the miracle will manifest?

Ishvara: Yes.

Why does the Virgin Mary manifest?

Ishvara: To open the hearts of human beings.

What happens after Our Lady has managed to open the hearts of human beings?

Ishvara: More positivity will happen in the lives of those who have opened their hearts.

Could miraculous healings also happen?
Ishvara: In many cases.

Even after the initial Marian apparition, could pilgrims who go to these sacred places be healed?
Ishvara: Above all.

But only if there is the consent of the divine plan can you be healed?
Ishvara: Of course.

How do we understand that there is divine consent?
Ishvara: You can only have faith.

Is it faith that generates hope for healing and gives us the strength to move forward?

Ishvara: That's why it's important to have faith.

How do we distinguish a real apparition from an illusion?

Ishvara: All apparitions are real for those who live them directly.

Many people visit the sacred places where the apparitions took place. How come if everyone could potentially experience them directly on their own?

Ishvara: Precisely because not everyone is allowed to have Marian apparitions.

In the case of the materialization of Vibuthi (sacred ash) on the statue of the Virgin Mary, what is that about?

Ishvara: The form changes.

Does this place also become a sacred place of pilgrimage and healing?

Ishvara: Always according to the divine plan.

Apparitions of angels or beings of light[18]

Some argue that those small bright spheres that sometimes appear on the photographs we take with digital cameras are signs sent to us by our guardian angels. In reality, there is no scientific explanation to date regarding the appearance of those spheres of light, most often associated with spirits or deceased entities. But it is not only digital cameras that intercept these spheres of light. Many people claim to have seen them appear while they were filming a scene with a video camera and to have therefore found them imprinted on the film; in addition, traces of these luminous spheres can also be found on photographs taken with cameras belonging to the older generation and operating with normal film.

---

[18] https://aiconfinidellanima.com/sfere-luci-angeliche/

Do guardian angels appear on photographs?

Ishvara: Rarely.

Can a place where many orbs appear be considered a place of power?

Ishvara: No.

It happened that some people took pictures in the same place, to some of them orbs appeared while others did not, why?

Ishvara: It depends on many personal factors.

Isn't everyone allowed to see orbs?

Ishvara: Of course.

Are orbs many light beings?

Ishvara: Yes.

What are they doing the moment they are photographed?

Ishvara: They are purifying the surrounding environment.

Do they also work through the image of a photo?

Ishvara: Yes.

How are angels manifested?

Ishvara: Mostly in visions.

What are their main messages?

Ishvara: Love, peace and brotherhood.

Are the characteristics of the archangels found in books correct?

Ishvara: Yes, although generalized.

What are the main tasks of angels?

Ishvara: To bring messages of hope.

Do angels make contact with us when we have lost all hope or are experiencing very dramatic moments in life?

Ishvara: Especially in cases of strong need.

Is it correct to say that everyone has at least one guardian angel?

Ishvara: Yes.

Could a guardian angel follow multiple people?

Ishvara: It is rare.

Are you a guardian angel who follows multiple people?

Ishvara: Yes.

Do guardian angels protect and guide us towards our soul mission?

Ishvara: Yes.

How can we communicate directly with our guardian angel?

Ishvara: By learning to meditate.

Should we increase our vibratory rate by meditating so that we can also communicate with angels?

Ishvara: Meditation is of paramount importance.

What can you tell us about the Ouija board? Generally, there is fear of its use. It is said that only dark entities can be contacted with it. Doesn't it depend on who uses the board rather than the board itself?

Ishvara: Only by those who use the board.

So, if someone who is using the board and attracting dark entities, this has to do with the person himself, isn't it?

Ishvara: Exactly.

Can angels also be contacted with the Ouija board?

Ishvara: Yes.

Being in a dual world, is it correct to argue that angels are in opposition to dark entities?

Ishvara: Yes.

Where is the guardian angel located?

Ishvara: In the light.

If we want to be in contact with angels alone, shouldn't we at the same time drive away dark entities?

Ishvara: This is what meditation is for.

Should one meditate to transcend both dark entities and angels?

Ishvara: Yes, meditation leads you to the source of your being.

What kind of angel are you?

Ishvara: It will depend on the situation from time to time.

At this time when we are channeling you to write this book, who or what are you?

Ishvara: The Absolute.

The Siddhis - Yogic Powers[19]

Siddhi is a Sanskrit term, used within Hinduism and Tantric Buddhism, which can be roughly translated to "spiritual power" or "psychic ability". It derives from the root Sidh (lit. "to accomplish", "to achieve") and, in the various Indian philosophical and religious traditions, it has assumed various meanings such as "power", "mystical perfection", and "ultimate fulfillment of life".

These skills can be innate or developed with to austerity and mystical practices.

Traditionally, eight Ashta are distinguished in Yoga, that is, types of Siddhi (although Patanjali's Yoga Sutra analyzes 68), divided into three categories:

- Siddhis of knowledge: Garima / Prapti (omnipresence)

---

[19] http://jivayoga.it/spuntini-yogici/136-potere-yogico.html

and Prakamya (perfection of desires);

- Siddhi of power: Isitva (supremacy over nature), Vasitva (control of natural forces) and Kama-Avasayitva (complete satisfaction);

- Siddhi of the body: Anima (become small as a atom), Mahima (become infinitely large), Laghima (levitation).

Physical and mental purification, for example, leads the Yogi to go beyond the limits of the five senses, thus achieving "occult" powers such as clairvoyance, divination of thought, enhancement of hearing, etc. In the Patanjali treatise we can see a double system, magical and mystical. Magical because it is based on the self-discipline of the Yogi in following the path of ascension, mystical because devotional, in that it provides concentration on God Ishvara, who reciprocates the "Ishvarapranidhana" (devotion to Ishvara), causing Samadhi or Ecstasy.

The major 8 Siddhis are:

1. Anima - the ability to shrink one's body to a minimum size;

2. Mahima - the ability to dramatically increase the size of one's body;

3. Gharima - the possibility of increasing one's weight at will;

4. Laghima - levitation;

5. Prāptih - the ability to obtain and materialize everything;

6. Prakaamya - the ability to fulfill desires;

7. Isitva - supremacy over nature;

8. Vashistva - the ability to submit anyone to their will.

These are the eight powers that could be awakened in the Yogi when his sadhana (spiritual discipline) is carried out with intensity and devotion. Siddhis are the psychic powers that could be awakened and acquired when the energy of the Kundalini flows through the Chakras, which are in turn activated. Thanks to the constant practice of Yoga, through the activation of the Chakras with specific Asanas to be integrated with Pranayama and the different Meditation techniques, the Siddhis can awaken within us, since these psychic powers are latent in every human being.

To each Chakra corresponds some Siddhis, which are more precisely:

1st Chakra: levitation - abolition of fear of death - mastery of breath and mastery of the semen - clairvoyance;

2nd Chakra: mastery over the senses, liberation from greed, envy, jealousy and agitation, vision of astral entities, superior intuition and ability to postpone one's death;

3rd Chakra: power to walk on burning embers (fire) and to master fear;

4th Chakra: wisdom of the heart, inner strength, balance of male and female energy, power to fly in space, be invisible and enter other bodies;

5th Chakra: serenity, purity and supreme knowledge of the Divine Law (the transformation of being into pure consciousness begins);

6th Chakra: cancellation of the Karma of previous lives, the auric field becomes so intense and vast as to transmit peace and harmony to those around us, here the Yogi has all the upper and 32 lower Siddhis;

7th Chakra: the state of Cosmic Consciousness is manifested, the Yogi has all the Siddhis but does not wish to manifest them, he merges into the Absolute, into God, into the unlimited universal and impersonal Consciousness.

.

When a serious yogic journey is undertaken, can the psychic powers of the Siddhis be achieved?

Ishvara: Yes, but it's not a rule.

To achieve the Siddhis must the 7 chakras be purified and harmonized continuously?

Ishvara: Yes.

Should those who own them use them for altruistic and non-egoic purposes?

Ishvara: Yes.

But if you use them for selfish purposes, what happens?

Ishvara: Everything comes back.

In any case should one always have a loving and respectful behavior towards others?

Ishvara: It is the foundation of every spiritual journey.

Can a Yogi who has achieved all psychic powers and remains humble be considered an Avatar?

Ishvara: Yes.

What do you do if you have some of these psychic powers but cannot use them because they are not required?

Ishvara: Nothing is by chance, it is only a matter of time.

Does this mean that sooner or later these powers will be required by the people who need them?

Ishvara: Yes, the people themselves will ask for them.

Can we also lose the powers connected to the Siddhis?

Ishvara: Of course, in case of inappropriate use.

Could anyone who acquired Siddhis misuse them?

Ishvara: The ego is always lurking.

What happens in this case?

Ishvara: The powers disappear.

What are the most important characteristics to deserve Siddhis?

Ishvara: Harmonizing oneself with the Multiverse.

How?

Ishvara: With meditation and self-knowledge.

What do you mean by self-knowledge?

Ishvara: Knowing yourself in everyday life.

How is this possible if we are continually distracted by everything we have to do and think?

Ishvara: Be increasingly aware of how you react to daily challenges.

Where there is no harmony should we try to become more kind to ourselves and others?

Ishvara: Yes, so you learn and grow evolutionarily.

And could Siddhis also develop?

Ishvara: Certainly not at the beginning.

What are the most frequent psychic powers?

Ishvara: Visions and clairvoyance.

And what can you tell us about materializations?

Ishvara: They are rarer.

Visions and clairvoyance[20]

Clairvoyance, or ability to see in the invisible worlds, is a latent faculty that will be acquired by every human being in the course of evolution and will give the opportunity to investigate facts such as the state of the human spirit before birth, after death, or in the invisible worlds.

Although this faculty is inherent in all human beings, an effort is still required to develop it in a positive way. If it were possible to buy it, many people would pay a high price to get it, but it cannot be purchased and there are no easy ways to achieve it.

There are two types of clairvoyance: one positive or voluntary and one negative or involuntary. With the

---

[20] https://www.rosacroce.it/la-chiaroveggenza/

former, the individual is capable of investigating and seeing in the invisible worlds with full mastery of himself/herself and adequate awareness of what s/he is doing. It is developed through a life lived in purity and utility, in which the individual is instructed to use it for the service of humanity. The second occurs independently of the will of the individual who sees what passes before him/her and who has no possibility of control over the phenomenon. The latter type of clairvoyance leaves the individual defenseless in the face of the possibility of a possession by a disincarnate entity, with the hypothesis that his/her life, both in this and in the other world, is no longer under his/her control.

It is difficult, if not impossible, to distinguish a psychic medium from a voluntary clairvoyant: the only element is given by the circumstance that no positive clairvoyant will ever ask for money or for any equivalent compensation, let alone to satisfy curiosity, but only for the good of humanity. The danger to humanity is understandable if the power of voluntary clairvoyance is used without discernment, being able to read the deepest and most secret thoughts of others. For this reason, those who aspire to acquire the spiritual vision must first demonstrate a lack of selfishness and not use these powers for personal interests.

Voluntary clairvoyance is the only secure means used to investigate occult facts and is the only one that achieves the goal. For this reason, the aspirant cannot follow the desire to gratify a curiosity, but only the selfless aspiration to help humanity. As long as selfish desires exist, no progress can be made in achieving positive clairvoyance.

In conclusion, only through voluntary clairvoyance can the individual carefully investigate the inner worlds and progress on the evolutionary path; instead, involuntary clairvoyance cannot be considered a reliable means of investigation and, moreover, leads to the undesirable situation of being controlled by external sources, with consequent evolutionary regression.

Is clairvoyance a gift we all have?
Ishvara: Yes.

How come it got lost?
Ishvara: Other priority interests.

What could clairvoyance be used for?
Ishvara: Greater clarity in life choices.

In the case of voluntary clairvoyance, could it happen to see unpleasant situations such as having contacts with kidnapped children or missing persons, or predicting the death of people through accidents?

Ishvara: Yes, and you can voluntarily close the perception channel.

What is the use of having these types of visions if they are not requested by anyone?

Ishvara: There is always a reason why they happen.

Should one always inform the people directly concerned about the visions one has had, even if these could be destabilizing?

Ishvara: Better to ask the people directly concerned.

Could people also be manipulated with clairvoyance?

Ishvara: Yes, for positive and altruistic purposes.

If the end is not a positive one, will we then have to deal with Karma?

Ishvara: Exactly, remember that, in one way or another, everything always comes back.

To become clairvoyant, should one always be honest and correct in order not to lose these skills?

Ishvara: This applies to all situations.

What other qualities should a clairvoyant have?

Ishvara: Sensitivity to the suffering of others and empathy.

Do extraterrestrials have the ability of clairvoyance?

Ishvara: Yes, more than humans.

Vibhuti materialization[21]

The materialization of Vibhuti is mainly widespread in India. Vibhuti (Sanskrit term) is the sacred ash to which supernatural powers are attributed. It is used for the healing of physical and mental diseases, since it materialized out of nowhere and since the ash is specifically associated with Shiva, it is also reverently called Kailasa Vibhuti or "Ash of the Kailasa", the residence of Shiva. Vibhuti gives prosperity, incinerates all sins, increases spiritual splendor, removes dangers and is an armor against evil spirits (it is in this way that the Vibhuti in Brihad Cabala Upanishad is praised, sacred texts written between 700 and 300 BC which contain teachings of the highest value and which were intended only for initiates). This

---

[21] Canalizzazioni di Angeli custodi, Spiriti guida ed Esseri di Luce, Dawio Bordoli e Maria Theresia Bitterli, Bod 2017.

sacred ash is also a constant reminder of the evanescence of the body, which in the end, after cremation, is reduced to an ash pot. Vibhuti has multiple meanings: existence, birth, success, luck and prosperity. This materialized sacred ash is a prasad (Sanskrit term meaning: divine gift, divine grace and purity) that heals and comforts, a symbol of the ultimate reality that remains after the shell of the ego has been burned by the fire of enlightenment, symbol of complete renunciation.

Vibhuti is also the evident manifestation of a superhuman and divine power, strength, energy that has in itself extraordinary properties of purification and the ability to ward off evil.

Ash derives its symbolism from the fact that it is the residue of combustion, what remains after the extinction of fire, and therefore means death and penance. Think of the Catholic rite of Ash Wednesday, when the faithful approach the altar and receive the sign of the cross with the ashes of the palms used on Palm Sunday of the previous year. The liturgical formula of Ash Wednesday is explicit: "Remember, O man, that you are dust and to dust you will return." In many other cultures, such as the Chinese, the Maya Quiché, the Musica or the Chibcha of Colombia and many others, the ash has taken on very important mystical meanings. Vibhuti is like a fine, grainy, or flaky powder. It can be fragrant or with a strong scent; salty or sweet or tasteless; white or blackish, or of intermediate shades.

Vibhuti, the sacred ash, represents the essence of Atman, the true Self that remains untouched by the bad (impurities due to ignorance, ego and action) and by the vasanas (attractions and repulsions, conditioning, attachment to the body, to the world, to fame, to worldly pleasures, etc.), which have been destroyed in the fire of knowledge. Consequently, Vibhuti is revered as a very important form of Shiva, which indicates the immortality of the soul with which the glory of the Lord is manifested.

Vibhuti is also connected to the Trimurti, to the highest divinity. The Trimurti (Sanskrit adjective; letter which possesses "three forms" or "three aspects") is a notion of the religious cultures of India which indicates the "three aspects" of a deity (deva) or of the supreme divinity. In the latter case, it is customary to indicate in the Trimurti the triple form of the supreme Being of Hinduism manifested in the three deities of: Brahma (the creator), Shiva (the dissolver) and Vishnu (the preserver), Vishnu who exercises his preserving power by means of the avatars (the most important being the heroes Rama and Krishna). Brahma is the male divinity and creator of all worlds and the first born of beings. Shiva takes on different forms and epithets. As lord of time he presides over the incessant dynamic creation-annihilation-regeneration, the rhythm is marked with his cosmic dance. In addition to being supremely powerful and destructive, he is also revered as a divine ascetic. The female divinity that often accompanies him is a symbol of his Shakti or vital energy. Vishnu is benevolent, preserving, and liberating God and is connected to the myth of crossing the universe in three steps. The abode of the Vedic God is in the highest heaven, which places him in a clear relationship with the sun.

Also, in the Bhagavad Gita, in the tenth chapter, there is a part on Vibhuti-Yoga which is the Yoga of the

Divine Manifestation. God is the source of everything: knowing Him is knowing everything; immanence and transcendence of God.

Sai Baba of Shirdi22 was an Indian mystic. Nothing is known about his birth. He is today one of the most revered figures in India, both from the Muslim and the Hindu and is considered as an embodiment of Love. His teaching was essentially love. A sacred fire is maintained lit still until today in the Shirdi Mosque, it is referred to as "dhuni", from which he gave sacred ashes ("Udhi") to his devotees before leaving. Ash was believed to have healing and apotropaic powers. Sai Baba of Shirdi, in fact, used the application of ash to treat the sick.

---

[22] https://it.wikipedia.org/wiki/Shirdi_Sai_Baba

Sathya Sai Baba[23], was an Indian spiritual master and preacher. Among the many performances of the great saint, one of particular importance was the materialization of the Vibhuti that he produced in large quantities for the faithful devotees. Among the other Sai Baba's "powers", documented with videos, there is "materialization" of gold necklaces, rings, and regurgitating from his mouth "Lingams" (phallic symbol and incarnation of Shiva) of jade but also of gold. Paramahamsa Vishwananda is also said to have these powers.

Why does Vibhuti materialize in certain places?
Ishvara: To help people who want to be helped.

Where does Vibhuti come from?
Ishvara: From the subtle worlds.

---

[23] https://it.wikipedia.org/wiki/Shirdi_Sai_Baba

Who materializes it?

Ishvara: Beings of light.

What function do light beings have in addition to materializations?

Ishvara: Transmitting messages and healings.

What is Vibhuti made of?

Ishvara: Organic material.

Why does it change color and smell?

Ishvara: Depending on the healing required.

The whiter the Vibhuti, the purer the people connected to it?

Ishvara: It depends on the source and the end.

Can Vibhuti heal everything if it is allowed by the divine plan?

Ishvara: Yes.

Does Vibhuti heal by cleansing the chakras and the aura?

Ishvara: Yes.

How do you take it?

Ishvara: Small doses.

On sick or wounded areas of the body?

Ishvara: Yes, on the third eye or drunk in a little water.

Is Vibhuti connected to avatars or ascended masters?

Ishvara: As well as to other figures of the heavenly hierarchy.

Are the places where Vibhuti materializes blessed by avatars, ascended masters and by the heavenly hierarchy?

Ishvara: That's why people go there.

How is it possible that some Masters materialize Vibhuti directly from the hands?

Ishvara: Everyone has his/her own task according to the divine plan.

What should be offered to the deities in exchange for the received Vibhuti?

Ishvara: Nothing.

Do we have to do ceremonies in these sacred places?

Ishvara: Only if explicitly requested.

Materialization of Amrita[24]

The Tree of the World, the "heavenly" tree is in particular relationship with its aspect of "Tree of Life". The fruit of this tree gave eternal life. The liquid that is extracted is identified as Amrita, "food of immortality", or the "elixir of life". It therefore appears more specifically in relation to what can be called the "vegetal" aspect of alchemy, in the same way the "philosopher's stone" is related to the "mineral" aspect. In short, it could be said that Amrita, the "elixir", is the "plant essence" par excellence.

We can find Amrita in liquid form, similar to honey, on the physical plane, thanks to the process of materialization. Amrita manifests itself when we

---

24 Ishvara Amrita Yoga: Il Nettare dell'Immortalità e la realizzazione del Sè, di Bitterli, Maria Theresia e Bordoli, Dawio, BoD 2019.

realize our original nature. It only materializes when a certain vibratory frequency is reached and if it falls within the divine plan. Amrita is among the strongest manifestations of the divine presence. Different scents may arise from it and, as also happens in the case of the materialization of Vibhuti, the texture and color may also change. Amrita has, as a basic fragrance, the rose scent, which helps open the heart. It works on the seventh chakra to help us access deeper states of consciousness. Those who ingest Amrita (a tip of a toothpick is more than enough), will live different experiences of deep peace and infinite love. Amrita also helps the regeneration of body cells. This means that the aging process can slow down. The Holy Grail, which is found in our heart, is the cup that contains Amrita. The Manna from heaven, mentioned in the Bible, also manifests itself as Amrita. The difference between Vibhuti and Amrita is that the former purifies, while the latter elevates the state of consciousness.

What is Amrita?

Ishvara: It represents the Nectar of Immortality.

Is Amrita the highest manifestation of divine presence?

Ishvara: It is among the strongest.

What is the highest?

Ishvara: The Absolute, the One.

Can Amrita have different scents like Vibhuti?

Ishvara: Yes, it can change.

How many times can Amrita be taken?

Ishvara: Only once a day.

How come when two people take the same Amrita they feel a different taste?

Ishvara: Everyone will feel different shades of roses.

What effect does Amrita have?

Ishvara: Works on the seventh chakra.

How come does the seventh chakra open?

Ishvara: To access deeper states of consciousness.

What will happen next?

Ishvara: Everyone will have different experiences.

What kind of experiences?

Ishvara: Of peace and love, except in some cases.

Which planet does it come from?

Ishvara: From the Universe.

What does it do?

Ishvara: It is similar to Vibhuti.

What is the difference between Vibhuti and Amrita?

Ishvara: The first purifies and the second elevates the state of consciousness.

Does Vibhuti represent male while Amrita female?

Ishvara: Yes.

What else does Amrita do?

Ishvara: It also helps to regenerate body cells.

And what would that mean for us?

Ishvara: It slows down the aging process.

Why should life be extended?

Ishvara: To best fulfill the Mission.

If we leave the physical body prematurely, should we reincarnate in order to accomplish the Mission?

Ishvara: Of course, the Mission must continue.

Isn't this also possible on other levels of consciousness?

Ishvara: They are not separate.

What is the difference between working in a physical body and not?

Ishvara: Without the physical body you are freer.

Does the physical body hinder us in a certain sense in carrying out the Mission?

Ishvara: On the contrary, it allows you to realize the Mission on the physical plane.

Is it necessary to realize the Mission on the physical plane? Could it not be done on a subtle level only?
Ishvara: They are closely connected.

Can we act without a physical body and also through other physical bodies that have incarnated to accomplish the Mission?
Ishvara: Of course, the work also takes place on the subtle planes.

And in a group as well?
Ishvara: Yes, unity is strength.

Why does Amrita materialize in a certain place?

Ishvara: To fulfill the divine Mission of healing souls.

Does this mean that in this case the Mission is beyond personal, but rather collective?

Ishvara: Yes, it is for a common good.

How does it materialize?

Ishvara: There are several triggers depending on the situation.

Do the Devas have something to do with materialization?

Ishvara: They are the primary cause.

Are they the ones who create it and then distribute it where it is decided by the divine plan?

Ishvara: Yes, they decide the way of materialization.

Why do they have this task?

Ishvara: To assist you in the evolutionary process.

What is the fate of those who receive Amrita and take it daily?

Ishvara: The divine sign of an important collective mission.

Materialization of rings and Lingam[25]

An Avatar always descends accompanied by great souls and by many of his/her Devas or Angels who incarnate with him/her, not always at the same time, some first, to prepare for his descent, others later to continue and spread her sacred message and support him in his great mission. Sri Sathya Sai Baba is called a Poorna Avatar, which means complete and endowed with all the powers or Siddhis that must accompany every true Avatar. The faithful consider Sathya Sai Baba a whole and complete Avatar with all the Siddhis (purnavatar), such as Krishna; the story was also covered by amshavatara Avatar, including Jesus Christ, Ramakrishna and Aurobindo. Contrary to other Indian masters - who regard miracles as belonging to a lower sphere - Sathya Sai Baba entrusts the proof of being

---

[25] https://quanticmagazine.com/archives/17/11/2013/quando-l-avatar-discende-sulla-terra-sri-sathya-sai-baba/

fully an Avatar to extraordinary signs or Siddhis. He offers his devotees all sorts of miracles, both in the psychic sphere (clairvoyance, prophecies, apparitions thousands of kilometers away), and in the physical realm. Sacred ash (Vibhuti) came out of the master's hands every day to which miraculous properties are attributed. The master was also considered capable of "materializing" objects of all kinds: statuettes representing various forms of God, gold rings, photographs, precious stones such as pearls and others that fell from above in the form of a sphere of light and materialized on the clothes after deep meditations or prayers, and in front of present eyewitnesses. From his mouth and sometimes from his hands was the sacred Lingam manifested, during a very important event, the night of Shiva or Mahashivaratri,. Lingam or primordial cosmic egg, "hiranyangarbha", symbolizes Lord Shiva, the God of dissolution - transformation, the destroyer of tamas or ignorance.

Why do rings or other types of objects materialize?
Ishvara: To dissolve Karma.

After a Karma has dissolved, does the object such as a ring, dematerialize?
Ishvara: Yes, that's why the objects disappear mysteriously.

How do you understand what message is behind each object?
Ishvara: It is the task of the object to transmit all the necessary information.

Could the object not dematerialize even if Karma has dissolved?

Ishvara: No, there is always residual Karma if the object remains materialized.

But couldn't it be used as a simple cult object?

Ishvara: Yes, then its karmic function changes from individual to collective.

What does a Lingam or Philosopher's Stone materialization mean?

Ishvara: The same as Vibhuti and Amrita.

What distinguishes them?

Ishvara: The source or the devas.

Is the Lingam connected to Shiva?

Ishvara: Yes.

What does the Lingam or philosopher's stone do?

Ishvara: Dissolve ignorance.

Is the purpose to know ourselves better?

Ishvara: This is enlightenment or realization of the Self.

To whom can the Lingam or philosopher's stone materialize?

Ishvara: To those who have realized the Self and that is foreseen by the divine plan.

What is so special about a Lingam?

Ishvara: The power to awaken supreme intelligence.

It is said that with the philosopher's stone it is possible to transform all metals into gold. What can you tell us about that?

Ishvara: It is symbolic of course.

What symbolic meaning does it have?

Ishvara: Turning ignorance into supreme knowledge.

What should be done with a Lingam or Philosopher's Stone?

Ishvara: In many cases ceremonies and rituals are required.

This only if specifically requested by a spiritual master, isn't it?

Ishvara: Yes.

For those who do not have this need, how do you recommend using the Lingam?

Ishvara: Listen to your heart while holding the Lingam on the third eye.

Can it also be used for healings?
Ishvara: Yes.

Are those listed above, all psychic or Siddhi powers that can be achieved?
Ishvara: Yes, omnipotence allows everything.

Whoever has achieved all psychic or Siddhi powers is considered a Poorna Avatar. What is the major power of the Siddhis?
Ishvara: The supreme love which is the love of thy neighbor.

Are you a Poorna Avatar?
Ishvara: Yes, too.

What is the task of a Poorna Avatar?

Ishvara: Spread love in any way.

Sacred and powerful places[26]

The Earth contains hidden treasures, places considered sacred because they are points of confluence of natural energies, places where harmony is created naturally: the so-called "places of power", areas full of a particular energy, which the ancients knew well, so much that they chose them to erect monuments and sanctuaries intended to harness and make the most of the beneficial terrestrial radiation. Over time, the Earth has been loved and honored by those who perceived and ascertained the power of these energies, and was teaching them to live in harmony and respect for these forces of creation.

In an archaic perspective, identifying a sacred space is equivalent to meeting a door, spatial or temporal,

---

[26] http://www.il-convivio.it/i-luoghi-sacri-o-di-potere

from which you can access particular dimensions. The initiate feels this passage, recognizes it on the basis of certain signs and uses it for the good of the community.

The sacred construction therefore fits into a suitably prepared space, where it often protects or welcomes a manifestation of divinity.

Before manifesting itself in buildings, sacred architecture originated at a glance, according to a procedure similar to that which allowed men to recognize connections and drawings in the starry sky, dividing it into constellations.

For example, those who have visited Stonehenge, the Great Pyramid, Delphi, Olympia, Paestum, Glastonbury or Chartres Cathedral in France will have perceived the strength, peace and harmony that these places emanate, attributing them to the beauty of nature and the building. This is certainly true, but there is something more: the energy of the place.

Now, when we talk about the magic of a place, we are referring to the intensity and type of psycho-magnetic field that distinguishes it from the surroundings.
The energy that vibrates generating this field is called psychic, even if it comes from one or more terrestrial currents, because in fact it is of the same kind as that produced by human thought.

To further deepen the understanding of what a place with a powerful magnetic field really is, one must realize that it corresponds to a point where the Earth, or rather the planetary consciousness of Gaia, expresses itself at the highest level.

A "place of power" is, as we have seen, a site of particular cosmo-terrestrial energy; a place that fascinates, where one would like to stay for a long time, where the mind becomes quiet and the soul is at peace. In these places, perceptible on a subjective level, the energy vibrations are also measurable with special instruments.

An Austrian architect named Purner dedicated himself in the seventies to the research and radio-aesthetic measurement of positive vibrations in hundreds of archaeological sites and ancient places of worship, some of which then turned into Christian churches.

He explains that the builders believed that terrestrial radiation could affect the atmosphere of places of worship and also the sensitivity of the people who attended them; and building in those places they wanted to make the priests surpass themselves. In other words, they wanted to help them make contact with the spiritual dimension.

The place of worship was therefore a tool to preserve that made natural forces even more valorized, just like a sounding board. In fact, in general, the altar or the point in front of the altar is a real sounding board of energy. The direction of the building and its structure and dimensions play a secondary role.

In conclusion, there is evidence that every time an individual enters a magical place she is influenced, first and foremost on the level of her emotions, while cases of phenomena that occur directly on the physical plane are much rarer and sporadic. However, it is obvious that the atmosphere of certain places is able to help make contact with higher realities, with transcendence. What drives us is a psychic current that raises us above our limited point of view, transporting us to places of thought where each being shows us her best qualities and everything is beautiful, harmonious, and complete.

Is there also a personal place of power? The personal place of power can be a place without prestigious buildings, inconspicuous or even modest, but capable of giving balance and serenity. It can also be a corner of nature, even your own garden: sometimes it can be enough to put yourself under a healthy tree and lean on its trunk to absorb the beneficial energy of the plant and feel better.

The veneration of sacred trees is widespread among all religions, with a preference for fruit trees that bring nourishment; tree worship probably preceded the stone cults (megalithism). It was to the trees that men made the first offerings and dedicated rites for the first time. The first sanctuary was therefore a forest in which nothing was built. Afterwards, altars were erected under the trees and this time intentionally planted the sacred woods in places with a high concentration of positive energy.

The symbolism of the tree and the sacred rock appeared and developed synchronously and parallel to the intelligence of man, as a natural necessity, in the most remote Paleolithic period. It began with symbolic designs, lines, geometric designs, then manifested itself with figures drawn on sand, engravings on rock, wall paintings and again with symbolic actions, gestures, dances and masks.

What is a place of power useful for?

Ishvara: It is a source of inspiration and healing.

Is a place of power a place where we feel in harmony with ourselves and with the Multiverse?

Ishvara: Yes.

Are there portals to subtle worlds in places of power?

Ishvara: Yes.

What happens when we meditate regularly in a place of power?

Ishvara: Heart and mind open.

In these places, is this opening easier?

Ishvara: Not only that, it is enhanced.

How do I recognize a place of power?

Ishvara: Staying there in meditation for some time.

By meditating for a long time in a place of choice, could this become a place of power?

Ishvara: Yes, there are natural ones and those charged by man.

What distinguishes them?

Ishvara: The second are stronger.

Will they be even stronger by combining them with places of natural power?

Ishvara: Yes, it will be an added value.

In places of natural power is it full of nature's elementals?

Ishvara: Yes.

What are they doing in these places?

Ishvara: They advise and heal.

If we meditate in these places where the elementals are found, can we then see them and communicate with them?

Ishvara: Yes, with time and meditating for a long time.

What attitude do they expect from us?

Ishvara: Respect and openness of heart and mind.

Are there also the Devas and the heavenly hierarchy in these places?

Ishvara: Yes, too.

Could extraterrestrials also be there?

Ishvara: Yes, but it is rarer.

Could a crop circle be a place of power?

Ishvara: Yes, but only if it becomes a place of meditation.

The most important characteristic that a place of power must have in order to become sacred is that one should gather to meditate?

Ishvara: Yes, meditation is essential.

Isn't a place of natural power enough to become a sacred place?

Ishvara: Meditation with time gives sacredness, energy and harmony.

Are places where Vibhuti, Amrita, Lingams and other sacred objects materialized, places of power?

Ishvara: Of course.

Did this happen because we regularly meditate in these places?

Ishvara: Yes.

What should the location of the Ishvara Center be like?

Ishvara: The most important thing is the meditation that will be practiced regularly.

What else is important for its creation?

Ishvara: Enthusiasm and collaboration.

Who will be the suitable participants for its creation?

Ishvara: Seriously motivated and trustworthy people.

Are these people already there?

Ishvara: Just a few.

Would these people be enough to start?

Ishvara: Yes.

Since there will be a group that wants it, could the right place arrive?

Ishvara: All of you will create the energy of the place.

When a group of people desires it, will the suitable place arrive?

Ishvara: Yes.

How can we recognize the right people?

Ishvara: From their motivation and above all from their concrete initiatives.

When the center comes, will people come to ask for help and healing?

Ishvara: The sacred place will attract pilgrims.

FREEDOM, LIGHT AND LOVE FROM ISHVARA

Bibliography

Books

- Channeling of Guardian Angels, Guide Spirits and Beings of Light, Dawio Bordoli and Maria Theresia Bitterli, Bod 2017.

- Ishvara Amrita Yoga: The Nectar of Immortality and the realization of the Self, of Bitterli, Maria Theresia and Bordoli, Dawio, BoD 2019.

Internet

- http://www.il-convivio.it/i-luoghi-sacri-o-di-potere

- https://quanticmagazine.com/archives/17/11/2013/quando-l-avatar-discende-sulla-terra-sri-sathya-sai-baba/

- https://it.wikipedia.org/wiki/Shirdi_Sai_Baba

- 1 https://it.wikipedia.org/wiki/Sathya_Sai_Baba

- https://www.rosacroce.it/la-chiaroveggenza/

- http://jivayoga.it/spuntini-yogici/136-potere-yogico.html

- http://www.inspiegabile.com/paranormale/fenomeni-parapsicologia-telecinesi-psicocinesi.html
- https://aiconfinidellanima.com/sfere-luci-angeliche/
- https://it.qwe.wiki/wiki/Marian_apparition
- https://www.padrepiodapietrelcina.com/stimmate-padre-pio/
https://www.letturefantastiche.com/poltergeist_fantasmi_vio lenti_fenomeni_naturali_o_altro_ancora.html
https://www.scienzenoetiche.it/raphael_project/inc_088.php
- https://www.lifegate.it/persone/stile-di-vita/i_cerchi_nel_grano1
- http://www.acam.it/extraterrestri/
- https://www.reccom.org/2020/02/17/triangolo-delle-bermuda-nuovo-colpo-alla-teoria-cospirazionista-ritrovata-la-nave-cotopaxi-scomparsa-nel-1925/
- https://www.notizieora.it/lo-strano-caso-delle-colline-magnetiche-ecco-in-cosa-consiste-il-curioso-fenomeno/
- https://www.focus.it/cultura/mistero/come-e-perche-la-mente-ci-inganna-polidoro
- http://tanogabo.com/il-miracolo-nelle-varie-religioni/

- http://www.oltre.online/2016/02/12/i-miracoli-indu-e-scienza-yogica-ashta-ma-siddhis/

- http://www.magiabianca.info/articulo.php?id=7

- https://portalemisteri.altervista.org/blog/le-sfere-di-fuoco-naga-del-mekong/

- https://www.focus.it/cultura/mistero/svelato-il-mistero-dei-cerchi-delle-fate

https://www.lastampa.it/viaggi/mondo/2018/01/14/news/sc operte-in-romania-delle-pietre-in-grado-di-crescere-e-riprodursi-1.33967347

- https://alienifranoi.wordpress.com/2013/05/14/il-mistero-della-fiamma-eterna-di-new-york/

- http://www.mondotemporeale.net/2015/12/sparizioni-inspiegabili-nel-parco-dello_28.html

Biography

Maria Theresia Bitterli

She has worked as a German and Italian teacher, translator and Italian-German interpreter for ATRA, Derman agency and several private schools, journalist for Tessiner Zeitung and Dr. Peter Hüttebräuker, Master of Art in Relational Counseling, Bachelor in communication science, constellator and imaginal counselor, drama therapist, music therapist, plays the harmonium and the harp, art therapist, master reiki, channelor, medium and light healer, Yin Yoga teacher, AyurYoga, Yesudian and Shamanic Yoga, astrologer (40 years of research), naturopath, spiritual researcher, together with her husband Dawio she created different personal and spiritual growth techniques such as Ishvara Amrita Yoga, relational constellations, Zen-Satsang, creative Zen painting, Ishvara-Meditation, Ishvara Healing Meditation and leads personal and spiritual growth groups. She has published 24 books.

Dawio Bordoli

Shamanic yoga teacher, imaginal constellator, music therapist, composer of music and spiritual songs as well as Zen music, master reiki, channelor, spiritual researcher, together with his wife Maria Theresia he created various personal and spiritual growth techniques such as the Ishvara Amrita Yoga, relational constellations, Zen-Satsang, Ishvara-Meditation, Ishvara Healing Meditation and leads groups for personal and spiritual growth. He has published 15 books.

ISHVARA

S/he represents the guardian angel, the guiding spirit of Therry and Dawio and of all those who feel it in their hearts. Ishvara is all of manifestation and, at the same time represents all that is beyond manifestation and, from their union there is the flowering of God, the Absolute, the unlimited universal and impersonal consciousness, the One, the emptiness, LOVE.

In the Sanskrit glossary (ancient Indian language) we find the following definition of Ishvara: the universal being, principle of every manifestation.

Starting from the Bhagavadgita, Ishvara becomes the title of the "Supreme God" and thus will be used, in the post-Vedic period, to summarize the different names of the deities.

Ishvara contacted Therry and Dawio for the first time on June 29, 2017 at 4.00 pm to teach those who request them. All of Ishvara's teachings have been published.

Since July 25, 2015 Therry and Dawio have been continuously experiencing different blessings and miracles of all kinds such as materializations of Vibhuti, Amrita, Lingham, channeling, visions, psychokinesis, clairvoyance and clairaudience as well as various other paranormal phenomena.

www.studioishvara.com